This Book Belongs To

....

Made in the USA
Columbia, SC
19 September 2024

42591828R00057